How to Be
TOLERANT

A Question and Answer Book About Tolerance

by Emily James

CAPSTONE PRESS
a capstone imprint

Are all of your friends exactly like you?

Do they have the same hair color?

Do they have the same kinds of

families and the same beliefs?

Of course not!

Being tolerant means being respectful
of the differences among people.

There are many ways
to be tolerant.

Lucy is a new student. At the bus stop, Aylah notices she looks lonely.

What should Aylah do to show tolerance?

Aylah invites Lucy to wait with her.

Being kind to someone new shows tolerance.

What can you do to show kindness to a new student?

Wyatt and Eli are playing
a word game. Wyatt is slow at first.

What can Eli do
to show tolerance?

Eli is patient.

Understanding that everyone works

at a different speed shows tolerance.

How can you be understanding?

Kate's favorite school subject is math.

Adam is having trouble with his math homework.

What can Kate do to show tolerance?

Kate offers to help Adam.
Taking the time to help
a classmate learn shows tolerance.

How can you help
a classmate learn?

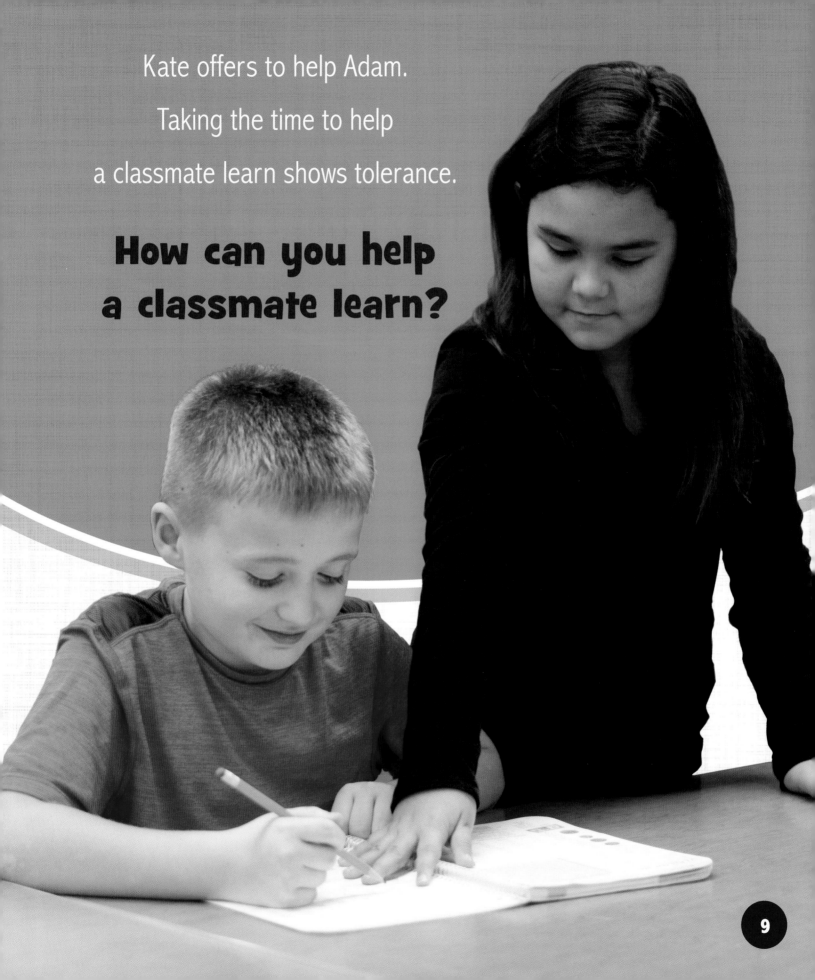

Aria and Adalyn start a club for girls only.

Owen asks if he can join their club.

What should Aria and Adalyn do to show tolerance?

Aria and Adalyn change the rules
so Owen can join. Including
everyone in a group shows tolerance.

How can you include others?

Dominic lives with his mom and dad.

Charlotte lives with her two moms.

How can the families show tolerance?

The families spend time together.

There are many different kinds of families.

Accepting other people's differences shows tolerance.

In what ways can you accept other people's differences?

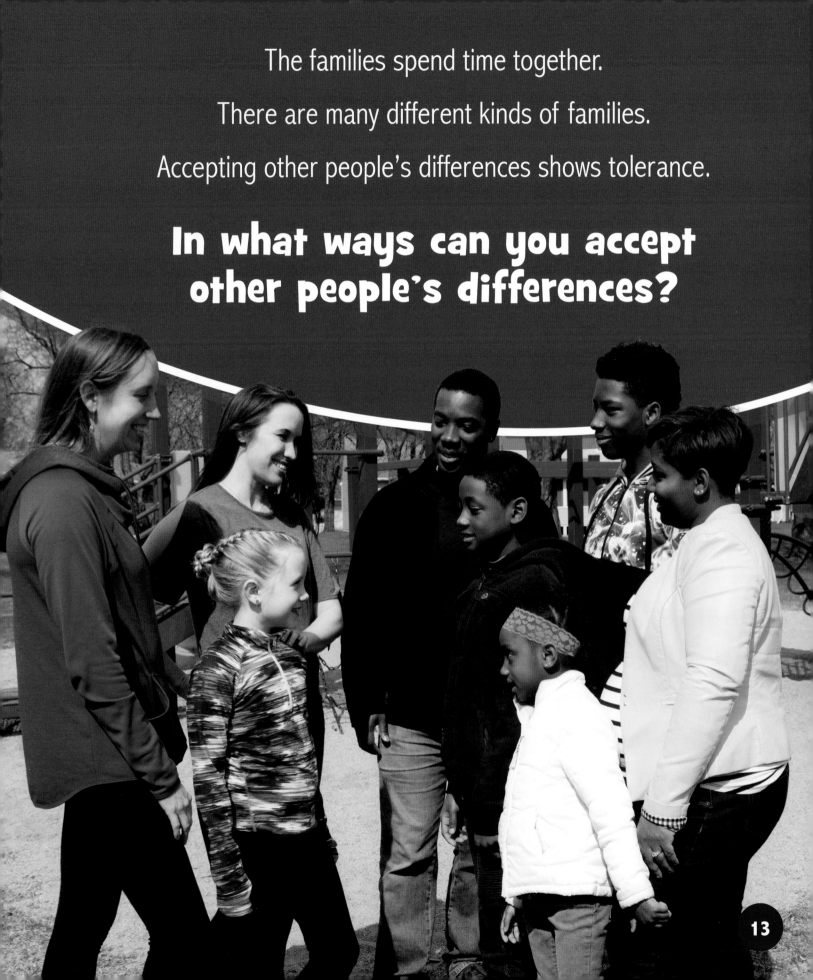

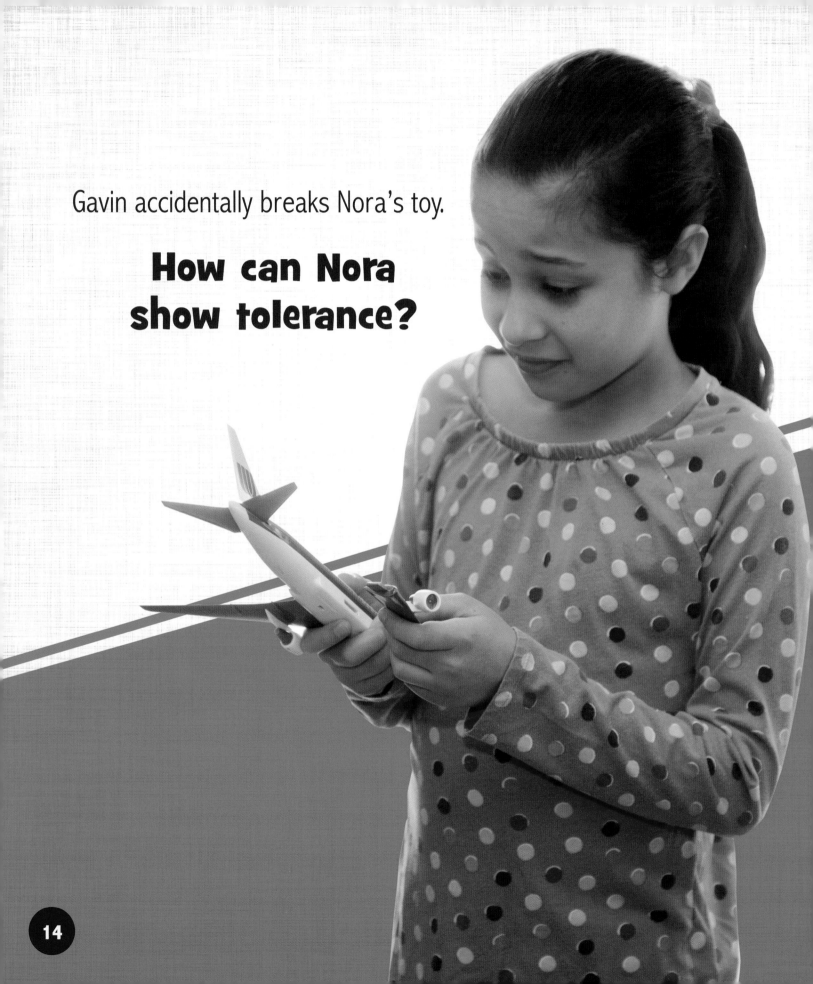

Gavin accidentally breaks Nora's toy.

How can Nora show tolerance?

Nora doesn't get upset. Never treat someone badly because of a mistake.

How can you show tolerance when someone makes a mistake?

Hannah's family celebrates Christmas.

Evan's family celebrates Hanukkah.

How can the families show tolerance?

They join each other for both of the holidays.

Celebrating other people's traditions shows tolerance.

What other traditions have you celebrated?

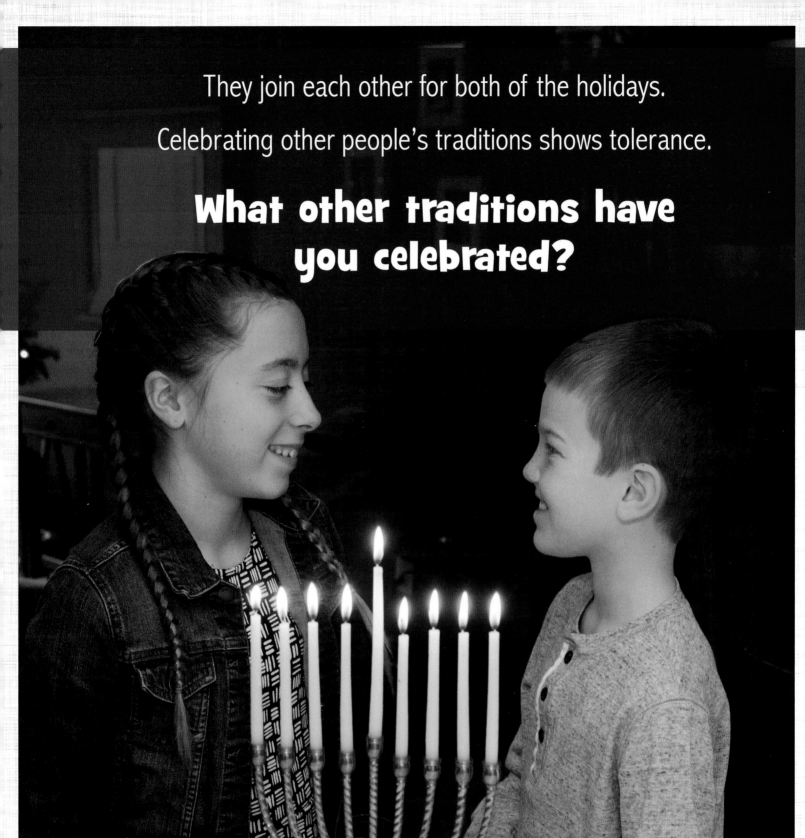

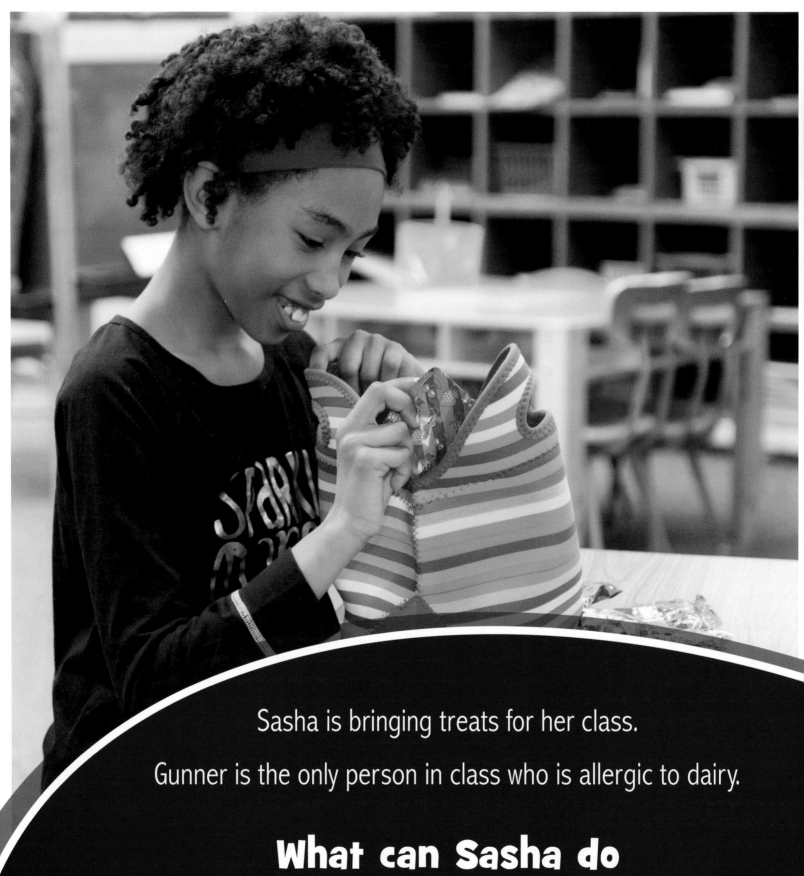

Sasha is bringing treats for her class.

Gunner is the only person in class who is allergic to dairy.

What can Sasha do to show tolerance?

Sasha makes sure to bring treats Gunner can eat. Being respectful of someone's differences shows tolerance.

What can you do to be respectful of someone's differences?

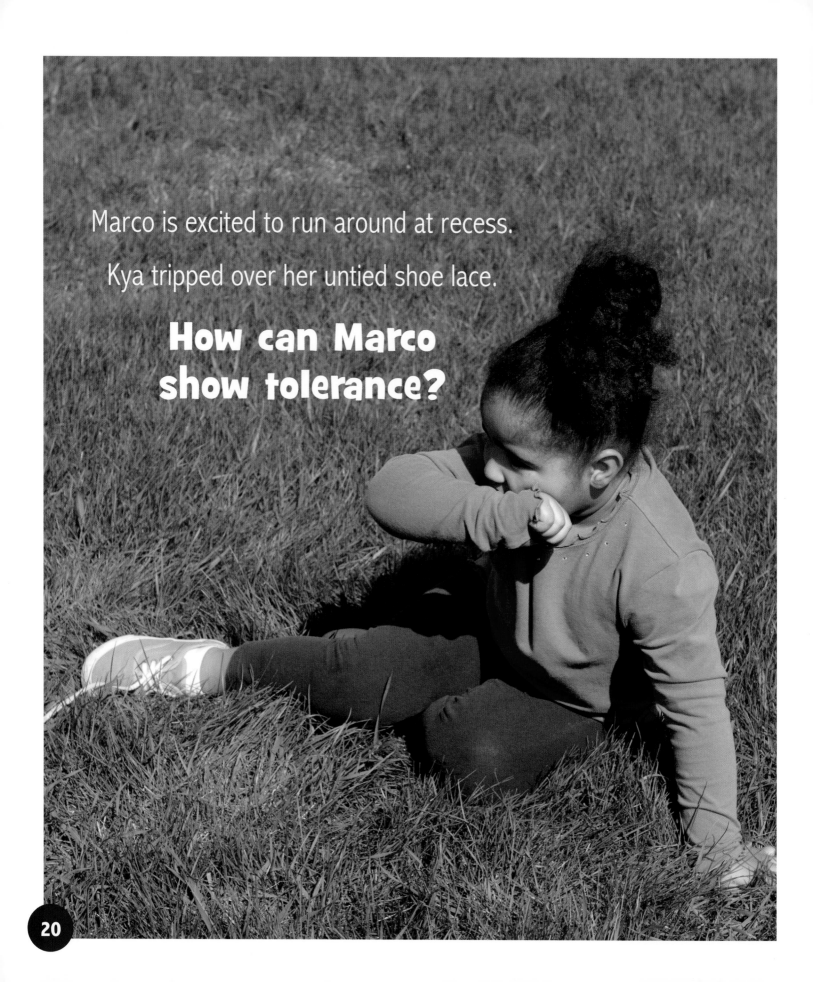

Marco is excited to run around at recess.

Kya tripped over her untied shoe lace.

How can Marco show tolerance?

Marco helps Kya tie her shoe.

Being patient is part of being tolerant.

Can you think of a time when you had to be patient?

Anna and Sasha are friends.

Anna loves cheering for her favorite sports team.

Sasha is a fan of another team.

How can the girls show tolerance?

They listen to each other's views. Respecting other people's opinions shows tolerance.

How can you respect people's views?

Levi's classmates are playing catch.

Levi is in a wheelchair.

How can his classmates show tolerance?

They ask Levi to play too.

Accepting everyone's abilities shows tolerance.

How can you be accepting of others?

Maria is new to the country. She dresses differently than some of the other kids.

What could other kids do to show tolerance?

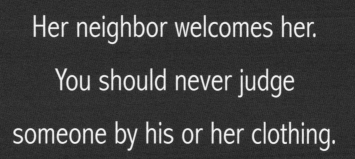

Her neighbor welcomes her. You should never judge someone by his or her clothing.

How could you welcome a new friend?

Olivia has to get glasses.

She is afraid her friends will make fun of her.

What should her friends do to show tolerance?

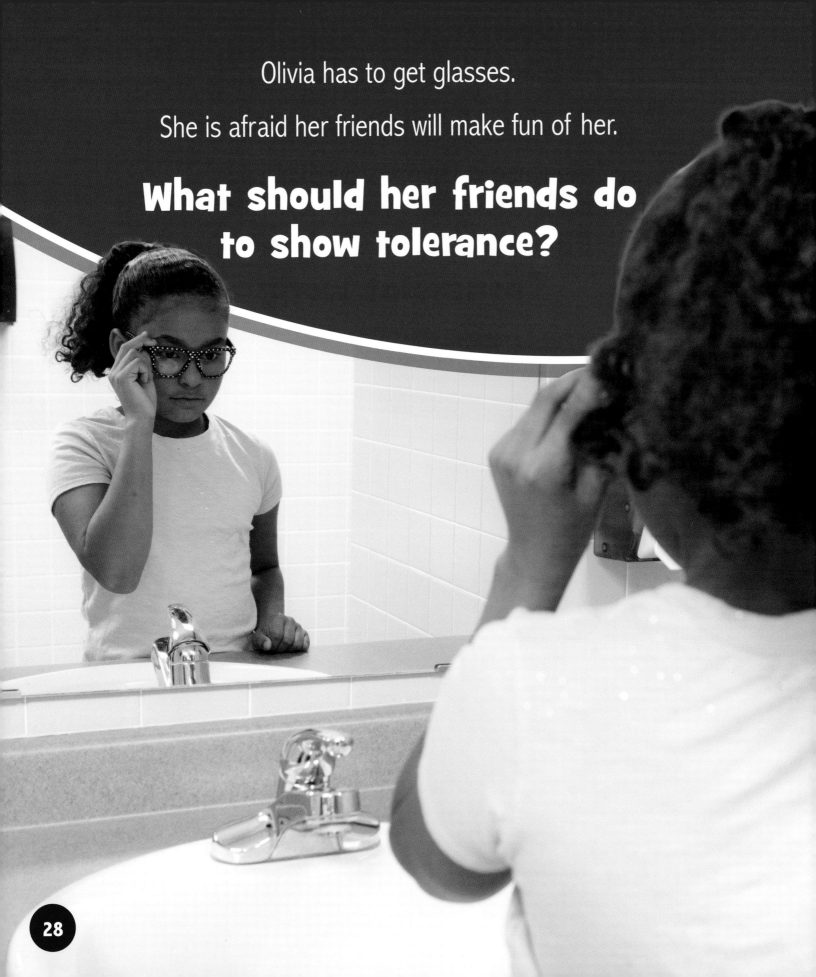

Olivia's friends tell her the glasses look great!

Treating others the way you would

want to be treated shows tolerance.

How do you treat others?

Glossary

ability—skill

accidentally—without meaning to

allergic—when something makes someone feel sick after eating, touching, or breathing it

candidate—a person who runs for office, such as president

celebrate—to do something fun on a special day

election—the process of choosing someone or deciding something by voting

opinion—a person's ideas and beliefs about something

patient—staying calm during frustrating times

tolerance—seeing that your way isn't the only way

tradition—a custom, idea, or belief passed down through time

Internet Sites

Use FactHound to find Internet sites related to this book:

Visit *www.facthound.com*

Just type in 9781515772026 and go.

Read More

Hanson, Anders. *Everyone is Equal: The Kids' Book of Tolerance*. What We Stand For. Minneapolis: Abdo Publishing Company, 2015.

Higgins, Melissa. *We All Look Different*. Celebrating Differences. North Mankato, Minn.: Capstone Press, 2012.

Newman, Lesléa. *Heather Has Two Mommies*. Somerville, Mass.: Candlewick Press, 2015.

Critical Thinking Questions

1. Owen wants to join Aria and Adalyn's club. What do Aria and Adalyn do?

2. Can you think of a time when you showed tolerance? What did you do?

3. Marco and Eli both showed tolerance by being patient. What does it mean to be patient? Hint: Use your glossary!

Index

A+ Books are published by Capstone Press,
1710 Roe Crest Drive, North Mankato, Minnesota 56003
www.mycapstone.com

Library of Congress Cataloging-in-Publication Data
Cataloging-in-publication information is on file with the Library of Congress.
Names: James, Emily, 1983- author.
Title: How to be tolerant : a question and answer book about tolerance / by Emily James.
Description: North Mankato, Minnesota : Capstone Press, 2017. | Series: A+ books. Character matters
Includes bibliographical references and index. Identifiers: LCCN 2016057034
ISBN 9781515772026 (library binding) | ISBN 9781515772064 (ebook (pdf)
Subjects: LCSH: Toleration—Juvenile literature. | Toleration—Miscellanea.
Classification: LCC BJ1431 .J36 2017 | DDC 179/.9—dc23
LC record available at https://lccn.loc.gov/2016057034

Editorial Credits
Jaclyn Jaycox, editor; Heidi Thompson, designer; Jo Miller, media researcher;
Laura Manthe, production specialist; Marcy Morin, scheduler

Photo Credits
All photographs by Capstone Studio/Karon Dubke, except:
Shutterstock: RoyStudioEU throughout, (background texture)

Printed In the United States of America.
032018   000236